TALES • FROM • THE
UNDERGROUND RAILROAD

Tales from the
UNDERGROUND RAILROAD

By Kate Connell

Illustrations by Debbe Heller

METRO NONFICTION BOOKBAG

METROPOLITAN TEACHING AND LEARNING COMPANY

Cover Illustration by Laurence Schwinger

Metropolitan Teaching and Learning Company
33 Irving Place
New York, NY 10003
ISBN: 1-58830-204-0

1 2 3 4 5 6 7 8 9 LB 04 03 02

Dedication

Alex Haley was General Editor of the first books in the Metro Nonfiction Bookbag. In this role, he provided editorial direction through all stages of book development, and wrote a special introduction for each selection.

Those of us who carried on with the project after Mr. Haley's death did our best to reflect his spirit in the stories. We hope that readers will find evidence of Alex Haley's influence on these pages, just as we felt his influence while completing them.

The books in the Metro Nonfiction Bookbag are Alex Haley's contribution to the education of America's young people. This book is respectfully dedicated to his memory.

Introduction
by Alex Haley, General Editor

How do you tell someone about the evil of slavery?

You can talk about the buying and selling of human beings, the cruel separation of parents and children, husbands and wives, brothers and sisters. You can describe the lifetimes of hard work for no reward. You can call to mind the violent punishments of whips, canes, chains, or worse. You can list the restrictions of the slave codes—which didn't allow slaves to travel, didn't allow them an education, didn't allow them to worship freely. That is one way to tell the story. Describe its horrors.

There is another way. Talk about freedom. Talk about how African American people, trapped in slavery's nightmare, dreamed of freedom. Tell how they did more than dream—how thousands risked everything, even death, to escape. Talk about those who succeeded. Talk about those who tried and failed but never gave up the dream. Celebrate, as *Tales from the Underground Railroad* does, freedom's story, and you will know that slavery is evil because it takes away freedom.

Contents

1

Independence Day, 1843

The sun had just dropped behind the horizon when Calvin Fairbank set out from the Little Rock House hotel. It was a warm summer evening. Fairbank headed for the river. He was leaving Little Rock, Arkansas, for good. The steamboat that would take him home left the wharf at thirty minutes after sunset, and he intended to be on it. The bright blue sky was already beginning to fade, and Fairbank walked quickly.

As he left the hotel, Fairbank fell in step with another man. This man—a Mr. Young—also happened to be going to the river, so they walked together.

They were an interesting pair, Fairbank and Mr. Young.

Fairbank was lean and fair. He was about 27 years old and had keen eyes and a long, narrow nose. In his plain, dark suit he might have been a minister. When he spoke, the people of Little Rock could tell he was not from around there. Fairbank was a northerner.

Mr. Young, on the other hand, was the picture of a Southern gentleman. He wore his black hair almost to his shoulders. His side whiskers and moustache were full and carefully brushed. His fine clothes and the gold-headed cane that swung by his side showed him to be a man of wealth.

So they walked, these two, making the kind of small talk people make when they have only just met. They passed people sitting on their front porches in the summer twilight. They passed boys and girls running barefoot in the dust. They tipped their hats to the ladies and bowed ever so slightly to the gentlemen. And no one suspected a thing.

No one suspected that Mr. Young's hair was really a wig. No one dreamed that his whiskers and moustache had been carefully glued to his face. Or that his expensive suit and gold-headed cane were borrowed, that even his skin color had been lightened with makeup.

No one, that is, except Calvin Fairbank. Calvin Fairbank knew all about it. It was part of a secret, dangerous plan. The object of the plan was to help the man calling himself Mr. Young to escape from slavery.

▼▼▼

Young's real name was William Minnis. Up until the year before, he had been living as a slave near Lexington, Kentucky. Then his master, old Mr. Minnis, died. Minnis left a will granting his slaves their freedom, but his son had other ideas. Like most slave owners, he saw his father's slaves not as people, but as property, worth a great deal of money. He wasn't about to be done out of it. He and the lawyers in charge of the will sold all the slaves, never telling them they were free.

William was 17 years old then. He was sold to

a slave trader who took him far away to Little Rock, Arkansas. There, deep in the heart of slave country, he was sold again.

Back in Lexington, William Minnis's friends were worried about him. They knew he had been sold illegally and taken to Little Rock. But that was all they knew. Then, ten months after William disappeared, his friends heard of someone who might be able to help.

All of Lexington was buzzing with talk of an antislavery crusader who lived across the river in Cincinnati, Ohio. This man had created a sensation at a slave auction. A glittering crowd of two thousand wealthy ladies and gentlemen had been there, and they saw it. Pretending to be a slave owner, the man had joined the bidding for a young woman. No matter what bid was offered, this man topped it. It seemed he meant to have her at any price. When he finally won, the auctioneer called out, "What are you going to do with her?" "Free her, sir!" the man shouted. For days people could talk of nothing else. The man was Calvin Fairbank.

So William Minnis's friends went to Cincinnati to find Fairbank. Fairbank listened to them. He agreed to go to Little Rock and try to find Minnis and bring him back. He had no idea what Minnis looked like or where he lived. He didn't know who had bought him. But Fairbank had his wits and his courage. And he had $250 that the friends of William Minnis had given him. That would have to do.

Fairbank arrived in Little Rock in the middle of May 1843. He checked into a hotel and began asking around for a young slave who had been sold there the year before. He had to be careful, though. White people in Little Rock were suspicious of this strange northerner asking questions about slaves. Could be out to stir up trouble about slavery, they said. Black people were suspicious of him because he was white and asking questions. Could be a slave catcher in disguise.

But Fairbank was clever. He worked slowly. He seemed not to pay much attention to the things people told him. Yet within four weeks he had made a discovery. William Minnis worked at the Little Rock House—the very hotel where Fairbank was staying! But which one of the servants was he?

Fairbank meant to find out. One evening he packed his carpetbag as if he were going to take a short trip to the next town. "Boy, see here!" Fairbank called to a servant. He used the same tone he had heard most white southerners use toward slaves. "Take this to the boat for me."

"Master, that's not my work. That's Bill's work," the servant answered.

Bill, thought Fairbank. Maybe he was on the right track.

"Bill!" the servant called. "See here. This gentleman wants you."

Bill appeared. He was a good-looking, light-skinned black youth of about 18. He picked up Fairbank's carpetbag and followed him out the door.

When the hotel was well behind them, Fairbank took his chance. "What is your name?" he asked.

"William Minnis."

Fairbank's heart jumped. Had he found him, just like that? A voice inside told him to be cautious. "How long have you been in this city?" he asked.

"Well, master, just about a year ago I left Lexington, Kentucky. I was sold to the trader, Pullum, and he fetched me here and sold me. I belong to Mr. Brennan, and he hires me out here at the hotel."

"Did your master live in Jessamine County?" Fairbank asked.

"Yes, sir."

"He died, and his son sold you, eh?"

"Yes, sir." William Minnis sounded surprised. "Did you know him?"

"Yes." Fairbank took a deep breath. "William, did you know Dennis Seals, and Nancy Straus, and Father Ferril?"

These were the people who had sent him to rescue Minnis.

"Yes, sir," said William. His heart was thumping now, too.

"Did you ever know that your master willed

you free before he died? And that your young master sold you, knowing all about it?"

William Minnis froze. Then his chest began to heave up and down. "No, sir, I did not," he managed to say.

"Go back with my bag," Fairbank told him kindly. "I'll not take the boat. Come to my room tonight as early as you can safely."

▼▼▼

That night Fairbank told Minnis everything. They talked late into the night. Together they came up with a plan to disguise William as a white gentleman and take the riverboat to Cincinnati. It was dangerous for both of them. If they were caught, William Minnis would most likely be whipped within an inch of his life. Calvin Fairbank would be arrested and thrown in jail. But with a little luck, the plan could work.

So it was that on the Fourth of July, 1843, William Minnis became Mr. Young. The real Mr. Young was a man who lived up the river from William's master. William Minnis had chosen Mr. Young to impersonate because he actually looked something like him. The wig went on, the false whiskers attached, and the makeup applied. Minnis put on the borrowed suit. He picked up the gold-headed cane and struck a haughty pose. The likeness was extraordinary!

With no time to lose, Fairbank paid his bill at the hotel desk and left. As if by chance, "Mr. Young" joined him. Within minutes they were aboard the boat. Soon the great engines gave a roar and the whole boat trembled. The steam whistle shrieked, the smokestack belched a great cloud of black smoke, and the boat moved slowly away from the wharf. They were on their way to freedom.

Then it happened. William Minnis turned to Calvin Fairbank and looked him straight in the eye. "Mr. Brennan is on the boat," he said. And there, among the throng of people that milled about the cabin, was William Minnis's master. Only one thing could save them now. "Put on airs," said Fairbank.

A moment later Mr. Brennan strolled by. Minnis turned.

"Mr. Brennan!"

"Mr. Young!"

"Oh! Fine evening."

"Very, sir, very." And Mr. Brennan walked on.

▼▼▼

William Minnis never saw Mr. Brennan again. He and Fairbank went to bed early, and by morning Brennan had left the boat to go downriver to Vicksburg, Mississippi. The disguise had passed the ultimate test. As they chugged north on the Mississippi River, Minnis and Fairbank began to feel safe. The worst was over. The danger was behind them.

But it wasn't. When the steamboat reached Memphis, Tennessee, passengers were told they would be stopping there for a few hours. No sooner had the engine died than up the gangplank walked Pullum—the very same slave trader who had bought and sold William Minnis! Pullum recognized Fairbank and went right over and greeted him. Soon their conversation got around to Little Rock, Arkansas. Pullum spoke of "a Minnis boy whom I sold there. Did you know him?"

"Oh yes," Fairbank replied honestly. "He is owned by Mr. Brennan—hired at the Little Rock House. He makes a good steward."

"Yes, he's smart," the slave trader agreed. "I made three hundred dollars on him."

Meanwhile, there was William Minnis listening to every word! He paced the deck a few feet away. Back and forth he went, swinging his gold-headed cane with an air of importance. Finally a bell rang to signal that the boat was about to leave. Pullum bowed politely, said good-bye, and left. Two days later Fairbank and Minnis landed in Cincinnati, Ohio. The first leg of William Minnis's journey on the Underground Railroad was over.

2

Traveling the Underground Road

By 1843, the year William Minnis escaped from slavery, the Underground Railroad had routes all over the country. These routes were invisible to most people. They ran through swamps and woods, across lakes and rivers, along dirt roads, down city streets, and through market squares. The Underground Railroad ran through slave cabins and farm kitchens. It ran through some of the finest parlors in the land. It went wherever there were people who hated slavery enough to do something about it.

It got its name from an old story about a

Kentucky slave who broke free and ran from his master. He ran as fast as his legs could carry him toward the Ohio River. When he reached the river's edge, he looked back and saw his master running furiously after him. The slave dove in and swam for his life. His master reached the river and hunted up and down the bank for a skiff, all the while keeping an eye on the man bobbing up and down in the water. When he found a boat, he jumped in and pulled at the oars with all his might. Before he reached the other side, he saw the man pull himself dripping out of the water and run into town.

The master landed and ran in the same direction. He ran to one end of town. He ran to the other. He searched high and low. To everyone he saw he put the same question:

Have you seen a black man, soaked to the skin, running fit to save his life? The townspeople just looked at one another. No, haven't seen him. Someone must have, he insisted, but it was no use. This was Ripley, Ohio, a slavery-hating town if there ever was one. Many a runaway slave had

dropped out of sight in Ripley. The townspeople stuck to their story, and finally the slave owner gave up. "He must have gone on an underground road," he said in disgust. He turned around and went home.

That phrase, "underground road," stuck. It captured the spirit of escape, something secret and determined and victorious. Black people took it up and passed it on. "He took the underground road" meant that someone had been helped, had gotten away.

Not long after that, the first steam locomotives were built. They were amazingly fast, faster than the fastest race horse. For the first time in America, the lonely sound of a faraway train whistle could be heard on the night air. It reached blacks on the plantations. It spoke to them of freedom, of leaving. Soon that "underground road" became an "underground railroad."

As years passed, more and more people got involved in helping blacks to run away. The Underground Railroad got bigger and more organized. People helped in whatever way they could.

Sometimes that meant hiding a group of fugitives under a load of hay in a wagon and driving them to the next town. Sometimes it just meant letting them sleep in a barn. It was risky, for even the smallest gesture of help toward a runaway was against the law.

Some people worked for the Underground Railroad and never met any fugitives at all. Abigail Goodwin of New Jersey was a poor, elderly widow. She had the kind, wrinkled face of a favorite great-aunt. She wasn't daring or heroic in the way Calvin Fairbank was. But she helped in her own way. She organized a sewing circle to make clothing for blacks who arrived from the South wearing only ragged slave clothes. She scraped together money and sent it to a friend of hers in the "railroad" business. She didn't know exactly what this friend did—it was dangerous to know too much—but she knew he would make good use of the money.

As the illegal network grew, a secret code sprang up. Runaway slaves became "passengers" or, sometimes, "packages" or "parcels." People like Calvin Fairbank who traveled with the runaways were called "conductors." The conductor guided the fugitives to the homes and shops of friends willing to help. These safe places were called "stops" or "stations." The owner of the house, the person who took the fugitives in, was the "stationmaster."

▼▼▼

When Calvin Fairbank reached Cincinnati with William Minnis, he knew just what to do. He headed straight for the home of the Cincinnati stationmaster, Levi Coffin. Levi Coffin was a white man and a Quaker. It was well known that Levi Coffin was opposed to slavery. Many Quakers were. They believed that God made every human being free and equal. Quakers had been lending a helping hand to runaway slaves for years and years.

Sometimes their other beliefs got in the way, though. For one thing, Quakers would not use violence, even when violence was used against them. That meant that they couldn't protect runaways from being recaptured by force. Also,

Quakers were not allowed to lie for any reason. So when an enraged slave owner came to the door and demanded to know if there were any runaways hiding there, a Quaker had to answer carefully. One Quaker woman, who had two young black girls hidden under the mattress of her bed, invited the slave owners in to search. "Let them come in," she said to her husband. "Thee knows there are no slaves here." She wasn't lying, for according to her beliefs, no human being is a slave.

At Levi Coffin's, William Minnis was safe for a while. His old friends came to see him, and they rejoiced together at his escape. But being just across the river from Kentucky put Minnis in danger. Cincinnati was always swarming with slave catchers. These were men who made their livings hunting down runaways in exchange for a reward. "Human bloodhounds" they were called. So with a new name of his own choosing, William Minnis—now John Crawford—boarded the Underground Railroad once again, this time for Canada.

John Crawford made it safely to Canada. No one knows exactly what route he took. He might have worked his way north to Toledo, Ohio, and then taken a steamboat across Lake Erie. He might have gone on to Michigan. From there it was just a few hours by train—a real train—to Canada.

We do know that he made it. In 1851, Calvin Fairbank saw John Crawford in Toronto, where he had been living for several years. His days as William Minnis were far in the past, where they would stay forever.

3

A Busy Day at the Station

It was the last day of May 1856, but in Philadelphia people were still waiting for spring to arrive. The sun was finally shining—the first time in days—but the air was almost cold. On Ronaldson's Court, a narrow alley of brick houses, a spindly locust tree bravely cast its dappled shade on the cobblestones. In an upstairs window, curtains billowed in a gust of wind and then an invisible hand shut the window with a bang.

If you had been there at a little after two o'clock, you would have seen the door of one of these brick houses open and a man step out. He was a handsome, round-faced black man, neatly dressed in a suit and waistcoat, bow tie, and hat. He stood on his stoop, drinking in the sunshine. Then, with a sprightly step, he descended the stairs and set off down the street.

William Still was returning to work after his mid-day dinner. He worked as a clerk in an office on North Fifth Street. But his was no ordinary business. His office was the official headquarters of the Pennsylvania Anti-Slavery Society, and he was their official clerk. Unofficially, though, the office was a stop on the Underground Railroad.

And, unofficially, William Still was the station-master.

Certain members of the Anti-Slavery Society had formed a special committee to help runaway slaves. They called themselves the Vigilance Committee. *Vigilance* means "watchfulness." When runaways arrived in town, the Vigilance Committee was ready. Its members took the runaways in, sheltered, fed, and clothed them. They interviewed them, listened to their stories, and helped them decide where to go next. For reasons of his own, William Still kept written records of these interviews. He was also in the middle of all the important decisions. For he was not just the office clerk. He was Chairman of the Vigilance Committee.

On this particular day, William headed back to work feeling more satisfied than usual. To tell the truth, he was quite excited. What a day it had been!

It had started before breakfast. Two runaways had arrived by the early train from Baltimore, Maryland. Their names were Harriet Eglin and Charlotte Giles, and they were two very resourceful young ladies. William smiled to himself, thinking of his interview with them.

Harriet and Charlotte had been house servants to two Baltimore gentlemen. No, they hadn't been badly treated. They simply wanted to be free. So they asked a friend of theirs who worked for the real railroad company, a free black man named James Adams, to help them run away.

Their plan was bold. First, Harriet and

Charlotte each managed to get hold of mourning clothes. Then, dressed in black dresses, black gloves, and long, heavy black veils of mourning, they made their way to the Baltimore train station. When they got there, Adams saw that they boarded the Philadelphia train without interference. He was a railroad employee and knew just what to do. He got them into a car, where they took their seats, bowed their heads, and looked—they hoped—too grief-stricken for words.

Just then a white man rushed into the car and looked around wildly. It was one of their owners! He hurried over to Harriet and Charlotte, who bent their heads even lower and made loud weeping noises under their veils. "What is your name?" he asked each one in turn, trying his best to peek under their veils. "Mary, sir," Charlotte sobbed. "Lizzie, sir," Harriet moaned. The man didn't look twice. He dashed into the next car in a fury, searching for his property. When he didn't find it, he left the train.

William was delighted at this story. He always took a certain satisfaction at seeing slave owners

beaten at their own game. But he never underestimated the enemy. Sooner or later the owners or slave hunters would show up looking for the two women. He decided that Harriet and Charlotte should hide at his house until all danger had passed.

But no sooner had they been packed off to Ronaldson's Court than another group arrived. Arrival number two was a black fugitive named David, about 27 years old. He was with a white woman and her ten-year-old child. This surprised the Committee. They had known of light-skinned blacks passing as white in order to travel freely. But rarely did white southerners, especially women, accompany fleeing blacks.

In the interview David explained that they had begun their journey in Leesburg, Virginia, in a hired carriage. The white lady posed as his owner, while he pretended to be her black coachman. This didn't raise any eyebrows in Virginia, but they had a scare when they reached Pennsylvania. The hotel owner in Chambersburg hinted to the woman that something looked suspicious. Finally he came right out and said that he thought the whole set-up was an Underground Railroad escape. But, he assured her, there was no cause for alarm. He wouldn't betray them.

David *was* alarmed. Suppose the man was lying? There was nothing they could do but keep going. They abandoned the hired carriage and the horse (which David had stolen from his master) and boarded a train for the rest of the trip. In Harrisburg they got instructions for reaching the Vigilance Committee in Philadelphia. And now here they were.

These fugitives, too, needed to be hidden immediately. The presence of the white woman and her child was no guarantee of safety. In fact, she was a fugitive now, too. She had broken the law to help David escape. But before the Committee could decide what to do with them, a third group arrived!

In the hectic rush that followed, William barely had time to write down anything at all. He quickly jotted down the runaways' names—Charles Ringold, Robert Smith, and John Henry

Richards—and their ages—all in their early twenties. They were all from Baltimore, all strong and able workers. The slave hunters were sure to be after three such "likely" runaways. The first order of business was to find them a temporary hiding place until something more permanent could be found. When this was done, William breathed a sigh of relief. He decided it was time for his dinner.

By the time William turned from Market Street onto North Fifth Street he was warm from walking. It was a busy time of day. Horse-drawn carriages clip-clopped along the cobblestone streets. People crowded the sidewalk, going in and out of shops, returning from their dinners, delivering packages, and otherwise attending to business.

William was still thinking about the fugitives when he reached No. 31. It was dangerous, having so many here at once. But he was proud of them just the same—proud of their daring, their resourcefulness, their spirit. Then he walked in the door and his stomach turned over. A police officer was there, waiting for him. With three new sets of fugitives on hand, this was not a welcome visit.

William barely had a chance to take off his coat and sit down before the officer began to state his business. It was this: He had just received a telegraphic dispatch from a Maryland slaveholder (Oh no, William thought), informing him that six slaves had escaped. (William felt better—none of his fugitives had come in a group of six.) The slaveholder had reason to believe the runaways were taking the regular train from Harrisburg to Philadelphia. (Was that a telegram on his desk? It must have arrived when he was out.) He, the officer, was ordered to be at the depot to arrest them all as soon as they arrived. A reward of $1,300 was offered for all six.

The police officer blurted all this out as though in a hurry to be done. Now he paused and looked down. William waited. The officer looked up and hesitated. "I am not the man for this business," he finally said. "I would have nothing to do with the contemptible work of arresting fugitives. I'd rather help them off." He looked down at the floor again, and then back at William. "What I am telling you is confidential."

It turned out that the officer had come to warn the Committee so that they could meet the fugitives at the depot and get them out of danger. William's reaction was not what you might expect. As soon as the officer confessed that he wanted to help the runaways, William grew more suspicious, not less. He listened and watched the officer's face with utmost care. He had to make sure it wasn't a trick.

The policeman seemed to be telling the truth, but William couldn't be sure. His instinct told him to open the telegram—it might be important—so when the policeman was finished talking, William tore it open. It said:

Harrisburg May 31st, 1856
Wm. Still, N. 5th St.:—I have sent via at two
o'clock four large and two small hams.

Jos. C. Bustill

So the officer was telling the truth! Of course William didn't read him the telegram. (The officer wouldn't have understood it anyway. "Via" was code for the Reading train station at Broad and Callowhill streets, which luckily, was not the station where the police were expecting the fugitives to arrive.) But William thanked him and let him know that everything would be taken care of.

That evening William met the "four large and two small hams"—or four grown-ups and two children—at the station. They had had a rough time of it. There were two men, two women, and two boys in the group. William learned later that they had stolen their master's horses and carriage and run away. First the carriage had broken down, then they had gotten into a fight with some white men, and then the horses had collapsed. They took to the woods on foot. For a week they plodded on over mountains, across streams, through thickets, eating whatever came to hand. When they arrived in Harrisburg, they were hungry, footsore, and weary to the bone.

But now was no time for talk. What if that

officer couldn't be trusted? The police would be hot on their trail. Greeting the fugitives in a low voice, William whisked them into a carriage and they set off down the street. He couldn't bring them to the office or to his own house or even to the houses of well-known members of the Committee. No, it was too risky. He would have to find someone else, someone sympathetic to the cause but not so well known to the police.

This was the most discouraging part of the whole day. William went first to one home, then to another and another. At each place, after learning of the danger, the fugitives were turned away. William tried not to waste time feeling bitter, but it hurt. The fugitives had risked everything for freedom. They had left behind parents, sisters, and brothers. And now to be turned away by people with plenty of extra room in their houses—people who in public had claimed to be "friends of the slave." It hurt.

Finally a widow named Ann Laws took them in. Her house wasn't so large, nor her food so fine, but she was good-hearted and willing to do whatever she had to do to keep the runaways safe. And now William Still could go home to his bed. He had earned his rest that day.

▼▼▼

Every fugitive who passed through the Philadelphia station on that last, hectic day of May 1856 reached freedom safely. Harriet and Charlotte, David and his white friends, the three men—Charles, Robert, and John—and the last six—all found shelter at the Stills' house or at Ann Laws' or somewhere else until the slave hunters grew tired of the hunt and went home.

Some three weeks later, William Still could be found, as usual, hard at work at the Anti-Slavery Office. Several letters lay unopened on his desk, and as he sorted through them, one in particular caught his eye. He picked it up with a smile and opened it.

Sennett, June, 1856
Mr. William Still: Dear Sir: I am happy to tell you that Charlotte Gildes and myself have got along thus far safely. We have had no trouble

▼

and found friends all the way along, for which
we feel very thankful to you and to all our
friends on the road since we left. . .

As he read, the image of two plucky young women in mourning flashed through William's mind. They had spirit, those two. They would do well. William felt a little swell of pride as he got to the end of the letter.

Please give my love and Charlotte's to Mrs.
Still and thank her for her kindness to us while
at your house. Your affectionate friend,
                                    Harriet Eglin

William folded the letter carefully and put it away.

4

Reunion

William Still was unique among Underground Railroad operators. He was the only one who kept written records of the fugitive slaves' stories as they arrived. Sometimes his records contained only the barest facts—names, ages, and where the runaways had come from. Other times he set down their stories in great detail.

Why did he do it? It was an extremely dangerous thing to do. The records contained enough evidence of illegal activity to put several people in prison for a long time. But William Still was no fool. He knew it was dangerous. He kept the records well hidden, sometimes in a graveyard and sometimes in the attic of the nearby Lebanon Seminary.

William Still had a simple reason for keeping track of the fugitives. He knew only too well how many thousands of black families were broken up and separated by slavery. It was his hope that the facts contained in his records might help sisters and brothers find each other and help children find their mothers or fathers. It wasn't an empty dream, this dream of reuniting families. He knew it could happen because it had happened to him.

When William Still was a little boy, he lived on a farm in New Jersey. It wasn't a big farm, just a log cabin in a clearing with woods all around. He didn't go to school. He didn't learn to read and write. Instead he learned how to swing an axe and fell trees and drive a team of oxen. He learned where to find huckleberries for the picking in summer, and cranberries in fall. And he learned something else: He learned that he was free.

William's mother taught him about freedom. In the evening, when chores were done, he sat before the fireplace and listened to her talk about the old days. Their family hadn't always been free. A long time ago, before he was born, his mother and father were slaves down south, in Maryland. His father belonged to one white master. His mother and the four children—William's older brothers and sisters—belonged to another.

William knew that his mother's name was Charity Still, but it wasn't Charity Still back in Maryland. It was Sidney. And his father's name was Levin.

From his mother, William learned how his father had gained his freedom. He never tired of hearing about it. "I will die before I submit to the yoke," was what Levin had said to his master. The words thrilled William. He pictured his father, tall and strong and proud, saying those words. The master listened. He set a low price on Levin's freedom. And he let Levin take on odd jobs—paying jobs—and keep the money he earned. Levin finally bought his freedom and moved north to New Jersey.

Sidney's master, Mr. Griffin, was a hard man. He would never let her buy her freedom, and even if he did, she could never save enough money to buy herself and her four children, too. But Maryland wasn't so very far from New Jersey. One day Sidney fled with the children to join her husband. They made it, too, but Mr. Griffin set the slave catchers after them. They pounced during the night, and Sidney and the children were dragged back to Maryland.

For three months Mr. Griffin kept Sidney locked in the attic at night. He thought this might cure her of running away, but he couldn't have been more wrong. Sidney hated slavery. She had seen what it had done to her father—seen it with her own eyes. Her father had died, horribly, when his drunken master pointed a loaded gun at his head and pulled the trigger. All Sidney needed was a chance, and she would run away again.

The chance came. After about three months, Mr. Griffin decided Sidney had gotten running away out of her system. She seemed quiet and contented. She sang church tunes as she worked.

So Mr. Griffin stopped locking Sidney in the attic at night. He let her go back to her cabin. A few weeks later, she ran away again.

This time, to her everlasting sorrow, she had to leave her two oldest, Levin and Peter, behind. Levin was eight, and Peter was just six. On the night she left, she knelt down by them as they slept. She kissed each boy good-bye and said a prayer. Then, taking one girl by the hand and the baby in her arms, she stole out of the house and headed north.

Sidney succeeded in finding freedom for herself and her two daughters. She joined her husband, and they moved to a different part of New Jersey where Mr. Griffin never found her. She changed her name to Charity. Together, she and Levin made a new life for themselves as farmers. They had fourteen more children—a large family, even in the days of large families. But Charity never forgot her two oldest boys.

▼▼▼

William was the youngest of Charity's children. He lived on the farm, doing the work of a farmer, until he was a grown man. He might have stayed and been a farmer all his life. But his mother's lessons in freedom had been learned too well.

In 1844, when he was 23 years old, William moved across the Delaware River to Philadelphia. He set about teaching himself to read and write. He joined the Pennsylvania Anti-Slavery Society. Before long they hired him as a clerk in their office, and he threw himself into the Underground Railroad business.

One hot August afternoon in 1850, William was alone in the Anti-Slavery Office, writing letters, when two men walked in. One was a black man about his own age, which was 29. The other man looked closer to 50. In the older man's face, William thought he recognized the hunted look of a fugitive slave. It was an expression he had seen many times before.

"Good evening, sir," the younger man said. William asked how he could be of help.

His companion, the man said, was from the South. He was trying to track down his family.

Was there a chance the Anti-Slavery Office might have his parents listed in some of its records?

William turned to the man with the careworn face. "What were your parents' names?" he asked.

"I was stolen away from the Delaware River," the man said, "with my brother Levin, when I was about six years old. My father's name was Levin, and my mother's name was Sidney; and we had two sisters . . ."

As the man told his tale, William listened with a feeling that he must be dreaming. For without a doubt, this was the Peter of all his mother's stories. It had to be.

The man only remembered that his mother had gone away one day, to church the boys had thought, except that by nightfall she hadn't come back. Then a man came along in a gig and offered them a ride. He promised to take the two little boys to their mother. Instead he took them to Kentucky and sold them. Levin had died nineteen years ago in Alabama. Peter—that was the man's name!—had bought his liberty and was now hunting for his family.

William kept his head. He would be happy to search the office records, he told Peter. But first he had to get some mail ready for the late post. As he bent to his work, he noticed that Peter moved closer to the door and stayed there.

When William was finished, he went to Peter. "It will take some time to look over those old papers," he said, "and this man may as well go home." William nodded to the young man who had come in with Peter, but as he got up to leave, Peter jumped to his feet.

"I'll go, too," he said nervously.

"No, no—stay," William said.

"Yes, stay—by all means," said the younger man. "It isn't worthwhile to go away now." And he left. Peter moved even closer to the door and sat down. He seemed to be trembling.

It dawned on William that Peter was afraid. And why shouldn't he be? He was far from home, far from everything familiar to him. He had been a slave for over forty years. His earliest memory was of being cruelly tricked and taken away from his mother. Why should he trust anyone?

As gently as he could, William asked Peter more questions. He needed to know what Peter remembered about his first home and his mother. Finally, looking Peter full in the face, he said, "Suppose I should tell you that I am your brother?"

Peter's face was a study in disbelief. "Supposin' you should?" he shot back suspiciously.

"Well, from all you have told me, I believe that you are a brother of mine," William said. Suddenly he was overcome with feeling. His voice shook. "My father's name was Levin, and my mother's name is Sidney; and they lost two boys named Levin and Peter, about the time you speak of. I have often heard my mother mourn about those two children, and I am sure you must be one of them."

▼▼▼

Peter didn't believe William. So William took him to meet his sister Mary, who lived in the city. Peter still didn't believe them. The next day Mary took Peter to meet another sister, Kitty, but Peter still doubted them. Finally they took the ferryboat to New Jersey and went to the house of another brother, James. And when Peter saw James, he knew they were speaking the truth. James looked exactly like Levin, the only brother he had ever known, who had died so long ago.

The next day Peter, James, Mary, and Kitty went to the family farm where their mother still lived. On the way, the children decided that, since she was nearly eighty, it would be better not to shock her with the news of who Peter was. They would wait for the right moment and then tell her gently.

Peter's first glimpse of his mother was of her standing in the doorway, waiting as they came up the walk. More than anything, he wanted to run into her arms, just as if he were six years old again, but he didn't. He came in with the rest and sat down to visit—a quiet, polite stranger. But when a silence fell, Peter broke it by asking, "Are all these your children?"

"Yes," she said, "the most of them are mine."

"You have a large family," he said.

"Yes, I have had eighteen children."

"How many have you living?"

"I have buried eight, and I have eight living," she said.

"I thought you said you had eighteen," Peter said. "Eight living and eight dead would make but sixteen."

"Oh," she said with a heavy sigh, "them two boys have been more trouble to me than all the rest of my children. I've grieved about them a great many years."

"What became of them?" Peter asked, his heart beating very fast now.

"I never knew what became of them," she said. "I left them asleep in the bed, the last time I ever saw them."

Then a strange thing happened. Charity's oldest daughter, Mahala, who lived nearby, burst into the house. She must have seen them all trooping in earlier.

"What is the matter?" she asked breathlessly. "Is anybody dead?" When no one answered, she looked around the room and her gaze lighted on Peter. "Who's this?" she asked. "Who is he? Isn't he one of mother's lost children? He favors the family, and I'm sure he must be one of them."

"Who, me?" Peter replied, flustered.

"Yes. Mother lost two children a great many years ago, and you must be one of them."

"I'm a stranger from Alabama," Peter said weakly.

"I can't help it," Mahala insisted. "I am sure you are one of mother's children, for you favor the family."

Then one of the sisters went quietly over to the mother and took her hand. Mahala's right, she told her gently. This man is Peter. He's come back.

Charity sat and stared as if her daughter had lost her mind. Then, without a word, she rose and walked into the next room. She knelt and bowed her head in prayer.

Within minutes she walked back into the room and went right up to Peter. "Who are you?" she asked, trembling.

"My name is Peter," he said softly, "and I have a brother Levin. My father's name was Levin, and my mother's name was Sidney—"

"Oh, Lord!" Charity cried out, and her voice

broke. Tears streamed down her cheeks. "How long have I prayed to see my two sons!" She went to Peter, and he put his arms around her as if he would never let her go.

5

Liberty or Death

Peter and Charity Still's happiness was a wonderful thing to see. For a whole week, mother and son talked and talked, getting to know one another again after forty years.

But the story doesn't end there. Peter's wife, Vina, and his three children—Peter, Levin, and Catharine—were still slaves in Alabama. Their owner, Mr. McKiernan, was a hard master to his slaves. Peter couldn't enjoy his freedom knowing that they weren't free. He decided to go back to Alabama and see if he could arrange to buy them. Every one of his relatives said no, it was impossible. He'd be risking his freedom and his life to go back. But Peter wouldn't be moved. "I can die," he said, "but I cannot live without trying to do something for my family. I must go back."

And go back he did. Not as a free man, though. Free blacks weren't safe in the state of Alabama. Peter went first to Cincinnati, where his former owner lived, and got a pass. The pass said that he was a slave traveling on business for his master. Then he took the steamboat downriver to Florence, Alabama. He went to the McKiernan plantation, only to find out that Mr. McKiernan wouldn't sell them. But if he did, it would surely be for no less than $3,000. At the end of November, Peter returned to Philadelphia. It was time to try the Underground Railroad.

Four months later, on a cold, wet night in April, William Still was working late at the Anti-Slavery Society office. The gas lamp cast a warm glow over the desk where he sat reading a letter. When he finished it, he sat back thoughtfully in his chair. The potbellied stove hissed, but William didn't hear it. He was thinking about Seth Concklin.

Seth Concklin was one of that rare breed: a white person who hated slavery more than he loved his own life. Back in December, Seth had come forward and offered to go to Alabama to rescue Peter's family. Seth was a stranger to the Stills. He asked for no reward. All he needed, he said, was expense money and some way to identify himself to Vina when he got there. He would take care of the rest.

Peter had refused Seth's offer at first. How could he ask a perfect stranger to risk almost certain death for his sake? It was too frightening even to think about. No, he would save his money and buy their freedom.

But that could take years, William said. McKiernan might never agree to sell. He urged Peter to accept the offer, and finally he did. And so, with $100 in his pocket and a gingham cape that had once belonged to Vina, Seth had left for Alabama.

A letter had come from Seth in February, and

another had come in March. He reported scouting up and down the Tennessee, Ohio, and Wabash rivers to find places to hide and people who would help. He bought a skiff and three pairs of oars. His plan was to row down the Tennessee River to the Ohio River, then up the Ohio to the Wabash River, to the town of New Harmony, Indiana. Thirteen miles from there lived a black farmer, Charles Grier, who would take them in. From there they would go another sixteen miles to Princeton, Indiana, to the home of David Stormon, a white Underground Railroad agent. At that point Stormon would take over, and Seth's work would be done.

Now this third letter had come. William sat with it in his hands, too happy to move or speak. Seth had written from Indiana—they had arrived safely and all was well!

It had been a hard journey, though. They had rowed for seven days and seven nights. Whenever there were people in sight, Seth had taken the helm and had the two boys row. The rest of the time Seth had rowed with them. It was grueling work, but in a way Vina and Catharine had it worse. They had to lie flat in the bottom of the skiff, covered with blankets. The water splashing into the boat kept the blankets constantly wet.

The first time Seth lay down under a blanket for a rest, two white men spotted them from shore and rowed out to them. Don't run, Seth told Peter and Levin. When the two men pulled alongside, they asked the boys where they were going and "whar from? Are you all black men aboard?"

Vina's sons answered, in the manner of Southern slaves, "White Massa lyin' thar, sir." Just then Seth got to his knees and threw back the blanket. He glared at the men as if irritated at being disturbed.

The white men bowed, as well as they could in a boat. "How de do, sir," they said and again asked where they were going and where they were coming from.

"To Paducah, and from Eastport," Seth replied in a dignified voice. The two men bowed again, gave them one last suspicious look, and rowed away.

Oh, it was a hard journey. "It would be impossible to describe the difficulties I encountered," Seth said in his letter. But they had made it safely to Indiana, anyway. Seth had seen them through. By this time, William thought, they are probably on their way to Detroit, Michigan. After that— Canada and freedom!

▼▼

A few days later, William arrived bright and early at the Anti-Slavery office. He had been walking on air ever since Seth's last letter. And his brother, when he had heard the news, was speechless with joy. All Peter's doubts and fears disappeared and he began, for the first time in his life, to think about the future. Soon he and his family would be together again, and what's more, they would be free!

William sat down at his desk and began to sort the mail. He hummed happily under his breath as he opened letters and put them into piles. Then, still humming, William turned to the papers. He opened the morning *Ledger* and scanned the front page. Farmers in Florida were trying to grow wheat. Eighty people had died of shipboard fever in New Orleans. A man in the next county had been crushed under the wheels of a carriage. How awful, thought William absentmindedly. And then he gasped. A small headline caught his eye: RUNAWAY NEGROES CAUGHT. His eyes raced down the page:

> At Vincennes, Indiana, on Saturday last, a white man and four negroes were arrested. The negroes belong to B. McKiernan of South Florence, Alabama, and the man who was running them off calls himself John H. Miller.
>
> The prisoners were taken charge of by the Marshall of Evansville.

No, no, it couldn't be! Don't let it be Seth and Vina and the children. But even as he prayed that it wasn't, William knew that it was. He put the paper down. He let out his breath in a long, heavy sigh. He should go see Peter right away. Peter would have to know. But William didn't get up.

He slumped down in his chair and closed his eyes.

▼▼▼

Not every Underground Railroad story had a happy ending. The dangers of running away from slavery and of helping others to run away were too great. Slaveholders were usually rich, powerful people, and the law was on their side. Even in the "free" states like Indiana, a runaway slave was still legally the property of the owner and if captured, had to be returned.

So Seth, Vina, Peter, Levin, and Catharine were put aboard a steamboat in chains, bound for Alabama. When they reached the plantation, Peter and Levin each got two hundred lashes with the whip. Vina got less than one hundred lashes, and Catharine wasn't whipped at all. As horrible as the whippings must have been, they were considered a light punishment.

Seth Concklin never reached Alabama to face trial. He disappeared from the steamboat one night and was never seen alive again. His body was found washed up a few days later, drowned, with his hands and feet in chains and his skull broken. No one will ever know exactly how he died. He was buried, still in irons, on the riverbank.

▼▼▼

The capture of his family and the death of Seth Concklin were a great blow to Peter Still. He grieved for Seth. But he didn't give up on his family. Not long after they were taken back to Alabama, William Still received a letter from Mr. McKiernan. In it, McKiernan offered to sell the family for $5,000. Peter spent the next two and a half years traveling through the North, telling his story, and asking for donations. In 1854 he purchased the freedom of Vina, Peter, Levin, and Catharine. So his story did have a happy ending, after all.

But what about Seth Concklin? He died trying to free four people at a time when slavery was the law of the land. In some people's eyes, this made him a fool, and a dangerous one, at that. But to many others, he was a hero. Because for thousands of black men and women life wasn't worth living if it couldn't be lived free. For them, and for those like Seth who helped them, there could be only one choice: liberty or death. Those were the ones who dared to ride the Underground Railroad.

Epilogue

Before the Civil War, the Underground Railroad was no more than a mysterious phrase to most people. Only people who were directly involved in helping runaway slaves knew how it operated, and they were bound to secrecy. What they were doing was illegal, so it was essential that their activities remain a mystery. Then, in 1865, the Civil War ended and the Thirteenth Amendment to the Constitution was ratified. It outlawed slavery everywhere in the United States. When that happened, the truth about the Underground Railroad could finally come out.

In the decades that followed, books were published in which former fugitive slaves and former Underground Railroad agents told their stories. The stories in *Tales from the Underground Railroad* were drawn from these sources. They are true stories. The people and the events of the stories are real. Some details—a screeching steam whistle, a soft summer breeze, a crowded city sidewalk—were made up. But all of the quoted dialogue that you read was given as it was reported by people who were present at the time. And the bravery, strength, and resourcefulness of the fugitives and their friends was very real.

So, too, was the freedom they earned.

Here is what happened to some of the people you read about in *Tales from the Underground Railroad*.

John Crawford (William Minnis) moved to California in 1852, after living in Canada for several years. When the Union army opened its ranks to blacks, he enlisted and fought for the Union in the Civil War.

Calvin Fairbank was arrested in 1844 and

again in 1851 for aiding fugitive slaves. He spent a total of 17 years in Kentucky prisons for this crime. In 1890 he published a book about his experiences as a conductor on the Underground Railroad.

Levi Coffin worked for the Underground Railroad until the Civil War broke out. He published a book about his experiences in 1876 and died a year later.

Harriet Eglin settled in the small town of Sennett, in Cayuga County in New York State. Charlotte Gildes went on to settle in Canada.

Railroad employee James Adams was arrested for helping Harriet Eglin and Charlotte Gildes escape. He went to trial in Baltimore and was found not guilty.

William Still worked for the Underground Railroad until 1860. In 1873 he published his Underground Railroad records in the form of a book. He also published two books about the black civil rights struggle. He worked as a coal and lumber merchant in Philadelphia until his death in 1902.

Charity Still lived on her farm for a few more years, and then moved in with her son, Dr. James Still. She died in 1857.

Peter and Vina Still settled in Burlington, New Jersey, where they bought a ten-acre farm. Their son Peter found work in Bucks County, Pennsylvania. Levin took up the blacksmith's trade and settled in New Jersey. Catharine moved in with her Uncle William in Philadelphia and started school there. Today, descendants of the Still family continue to reside in New Jersey.

Kate Connell lives in New York and is a freelance editor and writer. She is also the author of *These Lands Are Ours: Tecumseh's Fight for the Old Northwest* and *They Shall Be Heard: Susan B. Anthony and Elizabeth Cady Stanton.*